PRAYING WITH
The
New Testament

Compiled by
Philip Law

from the words of
THE GOOD NEWS BIBLE

Introduction by Joyce Huggett

TRI/\NGLE

First published 1988
Triangle
SPCK
Holy Trinity Church
Marylebone Road
London NW1 4DU

Second impression 1990

British Library Cataloguing in Publication Data
Praying with the New Testament.
1. Christian life. Prayers. Bible
N.T. Collections
1. Law, Philip, *1958*–
242'.5

ISBN 0-281-04343-4

Typeset by Rowland Phototypesetting Ltd
Bury St Edmunds, Suffolk
Printed in Great Britain by
BPCC Hazell Books
Aylesbury, Bucks, England
Member of BPCC Ltd.

PRAYING WITH
THE NEW TESTAMENT

IRENE BUCHANAN
3! The Hill, Thornhill, Stirling FK8 3PT Scotland

Other titles in preparation

Contents

An asterisk (*) following the Bible reference after a prayer indicates that the Bible text has been adapted or expanded.

Introduction

Prayer, like a precious diamond, has a variety of facets. Each could cause us to catch our breath in wonder. Each presses home the awesome truth that this gem-stone is priceless.

Down the centuries, different people have looked at prayer from different angles and highlighted different aspects of its inestimable value, so that now we are aware that, through prayer, the creature can so develop his relationship with the Creator that he can claim to know him, to be known by him and to be held in his love. In other words, we know that prayer is intimacy with God. But we are also aware that prayer is more than that. Prayer includes asking. It is the act of spreading before God the poverty of our need and emptiness and requesting that, from the abundance of his riches, God, the generous Giver, will respond to those needs in the way which is most appropriate.

And the scope of prayer is bigger still. Prayer is about seeking God and being found by him. It is about so gazing at God through contemplation or meditation that we are caught up in wonder, love and praise. And it is about making a personal response to the divine Lover. Prayer is all of these and none of them. Because prayer is bigger than each; bigger, too, than the sum total of these mere glimpses of the glorious jewel of prayer.

The disciples recognised that, of all men, Jesus was *the* man of prayer and so they begged him: 'Lord, teach us to pray.' That prayer is being echoed by countless Christians today for whom prayer is a hunger. And as we do what the disciples did: observe Jesus at prayer, it becomes obvious that his prayer life was saturated with the revealed Word of God – the Old Testament. Jesus leaned on this written Word for his authority, so trusting in it that he hurled it at Satan whenever the tempter tried to dissuade him from walking God's way. He was so steeped in it that, whether he was praying spontaneously as he walked the Galilean hills or whether he was screaming with pain, it was words of Scripture that flowed from his lips. So in the wilderness we find Jesus responding to every subtle ploy of Satan with that authoritative phrase: 'It is written . . .' (see Luke 4.4,8,12), and even from the Cross his anguished cries are echoes of Scripture. 'Father! In your hands I place my spirit!' is a direct quote from Psalm 31.5 and 'My God, my God, why did you abandon me?' is a replay of Psalm 22.1.

Why did Jesus rely so heavily on the revealed Word of God recorded in the Old Testament? How had these sacred Scriptures become so much a part of his vocabulary? What happens to the man or woman of God who seeks to emulate this Master pray-er? In discovering the answers to these questions, we discover several reasons why we owe a debt of gratitude to the compiler of this book of New Testament prayers.

Why Jesus prayed the Scriptures

One reason why Jesus' prayer reverberated with phrases familiar to every student of the Old Testament was surely that the Son of God recognised that this is no ordinary word lacking life and lustre. On the contrary, this is God's Word. 'That is to say, it is a seed of life that can strike root and germinate; it is a glowing coal that purifies and gives warmth; a spark that can set my heart ablaze like a dry haystack.'[1] Like the Psalmist, Jesus knew that God's Word was life-giving, life-transforming, life-reviving, life-restoring. This Word is liberating. It makes people wise, gives hope to

[1] André Louf, *Teach Us to Pray* Darton, Longman and Todd 1978, p. 47

the helpless, guidance to the perplexed. It beams its light into our darkness and feeds our hunger with a mysterious kind of food which satisfies so deeply that we crave constantly for more.[2]

And Jesus built on these insights penned by the Old Testament poet and showed us that our hearts had been architect-designed to receive this bread of heaven. André Louf explains the position powerfully when he emphasises that every Christian is indwelt by God in their innermost being. The same Spirit of God who has taken up residence in the temple of our soul also energises God's Word which comes to us from outside.

> From the very outset there exists an affinity between the Word from outside, awakening us, and the Spirit watching and waiting in our sleeping heart . . . When the Word of God accosts our heart, then suddenly and quite unexpectedly the one may recognise the other, thanks to the one Spirit who is present in both. A bridge is made, as it were, between our heart and the Word. From heart to Word a spark is transmitted. Between the Spirit lying dormant deep within our heart and the Spirit who is active in the Word a fruitful and vitalising dialogue begins.[3]

The Word thus penetrates to the very depths of our being in an almost uncanny way. And it generates new life in us.

J. B. Phillips discovered the truth of this claim when he set himself the task of translating the New Testament into modern English:

> I did my best to keep an emotional detachment. Yet I found that, again and again, the material under my hands was strangely alive. It spoke to my condition in a most uncanny way. I use the word uncanny for want of a better

[2] Psalm 119.50,92,25,107,98,114,130,105; Matthew 4.4
[3] André Louf, ibid., p. 39

word. But it was a very strange experience to sense the living quality of these rather strangely assorted books.[4]

The longer he pored over the New Testament, the more he was gripped by the realisation that these living words were inspired. He confesses that no other work made a similar impact on him. No other work he encountered seemed similarly in-breathed by God.

Was that why Jesus tuned into the sacred Scriptures with his spiritual antennae always at the alert? Was that why he referred to the Scriptures to support his own teaching? Was that why he reminded his followers of the words of prophecy recorded in the Old Testament and why he so exposed his whole being to this living Word that the prayer he breathed was shot through with the sacred text? We are not given answers to these questions but we may safely surmise that the answer to each of them is a resounding Yes. Similarly, we may assume that if we seek to emulate Jesus, our prayer, too, will be punctuated with words and phrases and concepts which lie embedded in the pages of the Bible. But if this is to happen, the Word of God must seep into the hidden crevices of our mind and heart and will and become a part of us.

How the Word of God becomes a part of us

And this can happen.

Before it can happen, the soil of our life needs to be purified and fertilised because, unlike Jesus, our hearts have been polluted by sin and hardened by self-centredness. The joyful message that pulsates through the New Testament is that, because of the death of Jesus, our sin-stained hearts and guilt-ridden consciences can be cleansed. And another message that throbs through the Bible is that our stone-hard

[4] J. B. Phillips, *Ring of Truth*, Hodder and Stoughton 1967, p. 18

hearts which are so slow to believe can be replaced with hearts of flesh which are quick to discern and believe God's activity in the world and the lives of his people. This purification and fertilisation of the soil of our life happens most effectively when we are silent before God and attentive to him. It is then that the seedlings of God's Word can take root and begin to bear fruit.

Down the centuries, men and women of prayer have discovered that, in this silence, there is value in showing ourselves receptive to the Word of God by reading a passage from the Bible as slowly as possible – pondering it, savouring it, turning it over in our minds, letting its truths trickle down into our hearts, waiting while it affects our will, our attitudes and, eventually, our behaviour. In recommending this slow reading of Scripture, Gerard Hughes suggests that we read a particular passage several times to see if any word or phrase stands out for us. Often some words will catch the attention of our subconscious minds long before our conscious mind is aware of the reason for the attraction, so it is important not to start to dissect the message. Rather, we must be content simply to drink it in. 'The process is analogous to sucking a boiled sweet. Do not try to analyse the phrase just as you would not normally break up a boiled sweet and subject it to chemical analysis before tasting.'[5]

As we assimilate Scripture in this way and abandon ourselves to its images we find ourselves engrossed by it. Like the Psalmist, we will harbour it in our heart (Psalm 119.11), cherish it (Job 23.12), cling to it (Luke 8.15) and embrace it (Acts 16.14).

And there is another way of ensuring that this will happen. The Psalmist sums up this activity in his

[5] Gerard Hughes, *God of Surprises*, Darton, Longman and Todd 1985, p. 47

telling phrase: 'meditating day and night' (Psalm 1.2). The word 'meditate' here does not mean a mere reflection on words or concepts. It means a constant repetition of those words; a persistent murmuring of them. Teachers of prayer have struggled to describe this activity by using a number of metaphors. St Cassian called it 'the rocking of the heart' which rises and falls like a ship dipping in the swell of the Spirit. Sister Margaret Magdalene likens it to a tumble drier. The heart 'tumbles and turns the word of God until it has made it its own,'[6] People in the Middle Ages used another evocative metaphor: *ruminari* – the *chewing* of the Word. Commenting on the aptness of this metaphor, André Louf suggests that it conjures up a tranquil picture of sleepy cows chewing the cud patiently and incessantly. Like those cows, he recommends that Christians digest and chew God's Word. Then rest before regurgitating and chewing the same phrase all over again. As we discipline ourselves to do this, we find that our aim is being achieved. This living Word will so penetrate and permeate and nourish and become a part of us that, when we pray, it will spring into our minds and flow from our lips with the same sort of spontaneity as it did with Jesus.

Some possible results

From this moment onwards, we will find that we are no longer lost for words when we pray because deeply ingrained in us, just as in Jesus, will be words of Scripture: those words which seem winged with supernatural energy and power. The Bible will furnish us with words which want to burst from us when we are brim-full with praise and thanksgiving:

How great, O God, are your riches!
How deep are your wisdom and knowledge!

[6]Sr Margaret Magdalene, *Jesus, Man of Prayer*, Hodder and Stoughton 1987, p. 97

Who can explain your decisions?
Who can understand your ways?
For all things were created by you,
and all things exist through you
    and for you.
To you, O God, be glory for ever!
(Romans 11.33,36*)[7]

The Bible will also furnish us with words which ring
with adoration of our Risen, Ascended, Reigning Lord
Jesus:

The Lamb who was killed
is worthy to receive
    power, wealth, wisdom,
    and strength,
    honour, glory and praise!
To him who sits on the throne
    and to the Lamb,
be praise and honour,
    glory and might,
for ever and ever! Amen (Revelation 5.12,13)[8]

The Bible will even provide us with words with
which to bless our friends and relatives:

I thank my God for you
every time I think of you;
and every time I pray for you,
I pray with joy.
My feeling for you
comes from the heart of
    Christ himself. (Philippians 1.3–4,8*)[9]

And the Bible will prompt us to pray quick 'arrow
prayers' in a crisis. With the prodigal, we might con-
fess: 'Father, I have sinned against you' (Luke 15.18*).

[7]See p. 30
[8]See p. 80
[9]See p. 37

Or with Jesus, we might submit to God's will: 'Father, not my will but your will be done' (Luke 22.42*). Such arrow prayers may also provide fuel for our contemplation and meditation as, with Thomas, we fall at the feet of the Living Lord Jesus and cry from somewhere deep inside ourselves: 'My Lord and my God!' (John 20.28), or with Peter, 'Lord, you know that I love you!' (John 21.16).

In other words, as we learn to pray the Word of God, the Spirit of God will hover over the chaos of the shallowness of our many words and the empty void of our wordlessness and create from them order and beauty, harmony and colour. Life. We may pray few words but they will be carefully chosen, weighty words, and we and others in our orbit will be enriched.

The joy of this compilation of New Testament prayers is that it makes it easy for us to pray God's Word because, under helpful headings, these living words are there, spread before us. As I have attempted to pray these New Testament prayers and to make them my own by reading them as slowly as possible and pondering them in the way I have described, I have frequently felt like an explorer who has stumbled on an oasis. And I have realised that the time has come to stop searching for a while and simply to rest and be refreshed as the Spirit who indwells me responds to the Spirit in the Word. So now my prayer is that those who pray this book will discover this richness for themselves; that prayer for each of us may not simply be the priceless gem which we hold in our hand but rather will prove to be the river bed through which the Spirit's life-giving, re-energising waters stream – particularly as we learn increasingly to pray the Word.

Joyce Huggett

Our Father in heaven:
May your holy name be honoured;
may your Kingdom come;
may your will be done on earth
as it is in heaven.
Give us today the food we need.
Forgive us the wrongs we have done,
as we forgive the wrongs that
others have done to us.
Do not bring us to hard testing,
but keep us safe from
the Evil One.

Matthew 6.9–13

PERSONAL PRAYERS

HELP ME, O GOD

Prayers for spiritual strength

Lord, I have faith,
but not enough.
Help me to have more!
Mark 9.24

Holy Spirit, help me

Holy Spirit,
help me, weak as I am;
I do not know how I ought to pray.

See into my heart,
and plead for me
in groans that words cannot express.

Romans 8.26–7*

Help me to pray

Make me, my God,
self-controlled and alert,
to be able to pray.

1 Peter 4.7*

Help me, my God, to be joyful always,
to pray at all times,
and be thankful in all circumstances.

1 Thessalonians 5.16–18*

No longer I, but Christ

Father, my Father!
Send the Spirit of your Son
into my heart.

Then I will live for you,
knowing it is no longer I who live,
but Christ who lives in me;
and that this life I live now,
I live by faith in your only Son,
who loved me
and gave himself for me.

Galatians 4.6; 2.20*

Christic in my heart

Father,
I fall on my knees before you.
I ask you from the wealth of your glory
    to give me power through your Spirit
    to be strong in my inner self.
I pray that Christ will make his home
    in my heart,
      that I may have the power
      to understand how broad and long,
      how high and deep,
      is Christ's love.
For by means of your power working in me
    you are able to do so much more
    than I can ever ask for,
    or even think of.
To you, Father, be the glory
    in the church and in Christ Jesus
    for all time,
    for ever and ever!
    Amen.

Ephesians 3.14–21*

Who will rescue me?

I am a mortal man, sold as a slave
    to sin.
I do not understand what I do;
for I do not do what I would like to do,
    but instead I do what I hate.
Even though the desire to do good
    is in me, I am not able to do it.
I do not do the good I want to do;
instead I do the evil that I do not
    want to do.
What an unhappy man I am!
Who will rescue me from this body
    that is taking me to death?
Thanks be to God, who does this
    through my Lord Jesus Christ!

*Romans 7.14–19,24–5**

I belong to you

Help me, O God,
   to avoid immorality;
to remember that my body
   is the temple of your Spirit,
   who lives in me;
that I do not belong to myself
   but to you,
   and for your glory.

1 Corinthians 6.18–20*

Help me, O God

Help me, O God,
to grow in the grace
    and knowledge
    of my Lord and Saviour
    Jesus Christ.
To him be the glory,
now and for ever!
Amen.

2 Peter 3.18*

Let me not worry

Lord Jesus,
Let me not worry about the food and drink
   I need to stay alive,
    or about clothes for my body.
Help me to see that life is worth
   far more than food,
    and the body more than clothes.
Increase my faith in my Father in heaven
   who knows that I need all these things.
Increase my faith, that I may be concerned
   above everything else
   with his kingdom
   and with what he requires of me.

Matthew 6.25,32–3*

Make me strong

Gracious Father,
fill me with the knowledge of your will,
with all the wisdom and understanding
    that your Spirit gives.
Then I will be able to live as you want
and will always do what pleases you.

Make me strong with all the strength
    which comes from your glorious power;
For you have rescued me from the power
    of darkness
and brought me safe into the kingdom
    of your dear Son.

Colossians 1.9–13*

When I am weak

I pray, O Lord,
   that I will not
   fall into temptation;
for the spirit is willing,
   but the flesh is weak.

Matthew 26.41*

Your grace, O Lord,
   is all I need;
for your power is strongest
   when I am weak.

2 Corinthians 12.9*

Give me your peace

Lord,
Give me your peace,
even though it is far beyond
    my understanding.
May it keep my heart in union
    with Christ.
May it fill my mind with
    those things that are good
    and that deserve praise:
    things that are true,
    noble, right, pure, lovely,
    and honourable.
Give me your peace, Lord,
    and may it always
    be with me.

Philippians 4.7–9*

Arrow Prayers

Father, I have sinned against you.

Luke 15.18*

God, have pity on me, a sinner!

Luke 18.13

Jesus! Take pity on me!

Mark 10.47

Save me, Lord!

Matthew 14.30

I believe, Lord!

John 9.3

My Lord and my God!

John 20.28

Lord, you know that I love you!

John 21.16

What shall I do, Lord?

Acts 22.10

Lord, you have the words that
  give eternal life.
You are the Holy One from God.

John 6.68–9*

Father, not my will
but your will be done.

Luke 22.42*

Father!
In your hands I place my spirit!

Luke 23.46

Remember me, Jesus,
when you come as King!

Luke 23.42

Lord Jesus,
receive my spirit!

Acts 7.59

TEACH ME HOW TO LOVE

Prayers for righteous action

Let my love be true,
showing itself in action.
1 John 3.18*

You are the only Lord!

O Lord, my God,
You are the only Lord!
I love you with all my heart,
    with all my soul,
    with all my mind,
    and with all my strength.
Help me to show how much I love you
    by loving my neighbour
    as I love myself.

*Mark 12.29–31**

Teach me how to love

Merciful Father,
teach me how to love my enemies:
    to do good to those who hate me,
    to bless those who curse me,
    and pray for those who ill-treat me.
May I be ready to give
    to everyone who asks.
May I always do for others
    what I want them to do for me.

Luke 6.27–31*

Transform me inwardly

Merciful God,
I offer myself as a living sacrifice;
I dedicate myself to your service.

Let me not conform to the standards of
    this world;
but transform me inwardly,
that I may know your will –
what is good and pleasing and perfect.

Let me not think of myself more highly
    than I should;
but let me be modest in my thinking,
and judge myself according to the amount
    of faith you have given me.

May my love be completely sincere;
may I hate what is evil,
and hold on to what is good.

May my hope keep me joyful;
may I be patient in troubles,
and pray at all times.

Help me to bless those who persecute me,
to be happy with those who are happy,
to weep with those who weep.

Help me to have the same concern for
    everyone,
to be humble and peaceful,
and never take revenge.

Let me not be defeated by evil;
but let me conquer evil with good.

Romans 12.1–3,9–21*

For the good of others

Dear God,
I desire to use for the good of others
the special gift I have received
    from you,
so that in all things praise may be
    given to you
through Jesus Christ,
to whom belong glory and power
    for ever and ever. Amen.

1 Peter 4.10–11*

The gift of love

I pray, Lord, for the gift of love;
　for if I have no love, I am nothing.
May my love be patient and kind,
　not jealous or conceited or proud.
May it not be ill-mannered or selfish
　or irritable.
Let it not keep a record of wrongs.
Let it not be happy with evil,
　but let it be happy with the truth.
May my love never give up;
　and may its faith, hope, and
　patience never fail.
May my love be eternal.

1 Corinthians 13.2,4–8*

Lord,
Let me not love in just words and talk;
but let my love be true,
showing itself in action.

1 John 3.18*

If I become angry

Father, if I become angry,
do not let my anger lead me into sin;
do not let me use harmful words,
    but words that build up and do good
    to those who hear me;
and do not let me make your Holy Spirit sad.
Help me to get rid of all
    bitterness and hate;
help me to be kind and tender-hearted;
and help me to forgive,
    as you have forgiven me through Christ.

Ephesians 4.26, 29–32*

Father,
make me quick to listen,
but slow to speak
and slow to become angry.

James 1.19*

Help me to help

Dear Father,
Help me, in all my troubles,
so that I am able to help others
  who have all kinds of troubles,
using the same help that I myself
  have received from you.

2 Corinthians 1.4*

Dear Father,
As often as I have the chance,
let me do good to everyone,
and especially to those who belong
  to my family in the faith.

Galatians 6.10*

O Christ, you are my example!

O Christ, you suffered for me
  and left me your example, that I may follow
  in your steps.

O Christ, you are my example!

You committed no sin,
  and no one ever heard a lie come from
  your lips.

O Christ, you are my example!

When you were insulted,
  you did not answer back with an insult.

O Christ, you are my example!

When you suffered,
  you did not threaten, but placed your hope
  in God, the righteous Judge.

O Christ, you are my example!

You carried my sins in your body to the cross,
  so that I might die to sin
  and live for righteousness.

O Christ, you are my example!

I was like a sheep that had lost its way,
  but now you have brought me back
  to follow you, the Shepherd and
  and Keeper of my soul.

O Christ, you are my example!

1 Peter 2.21–5*

THANKS BE TO GOD!

Prayers of thanksgiving

My heart praises the Lord;
my soul is glad because of God
my Saviour.
Luke 1.46–7

Lord of heaven and earth

Father, Lord of heaven and earth!
I thank you because you have given all things
    to your Son.
No one knows the Son except the Father,
and no one knows the Father except the Son
and those to whom the Son chooses to
    reveal him.
Father, Lord of heaven and earth!
I thank you.

Matthew 11.25,7*

I have become rich

My God, I give thanks to you
    for the grace you have given me
    through Christ.
In union with him
    I have become rich in all things.

1 Corinthians 1.4–5*

To you, O God, be the glory

How great, O God, are your riches!
How deep are your wisdom and knowledge!
Who can explain your decisions?
Who can understand your ways?
For all things were created by you,
and all things exist through you
    and for you.
To you, O God, be the glory for ever!
Amen.

Romans 11.33,36*

In the name of Jesus

Lord Jesus,
Everything I do or say
I do in your name,
as I give thanks
through you
to God the Father.

Colossians 3.17*

The Lord will rescue me

The Lord will rescue me
   from all evil
and take me safely into his
   heavenly Kingdom.
To him be the glory for ever
   and ever! Amen.

2 Timothy 4.18

Arrow Praises

Thanks be to God!

Romans 6.17

Blessed be his name for ever!

2 Corinthians 11.31

May God, who rules over all,
be praised for ever! Amen.

Romans 9.5

I thank you, Father,
that you listen to me.

John 11.41

Father,
bring glory to your name!

John 12.28

PEACE BE WITH YOU

Prayers of blessing

May grace and peace be yours.
1 Thessalonians 1.1

Joy and peace

May God, the source of hope,
fill you with all joy and peace
by means of your faith in him,
so that your hope will continue
    to grow
by the power of the Holy Spirit.

Romans 15.13

From the heart of Christ

I thank my God for you
every time I think of you;
and every time I pray for you,
I pray with joy.
My feeling for you
comes from the heart of
    Christ himself.

Philippians 1.3–4,8*

Knowledge and judgement

I pray that your love will keep on
    growing more and more,
with true knowledge and perfect
    judgement,
so that you will be able to choose
    what is best
and be free from all
    impurity and blame
    on the Day of Christ.

Philippians 1.9–10*

Free from every fault

May the God who gives us peace
make you holy in every way
and keep your whole being –
spirit, soul, and body –
free from every fault
at the coming of our Lord
   Jesus Christ.

1 Thessalonians 5.23

Love and endurance

May the Lord lead you
   into a greater understanding
   of God's love
and the endurance that is
   given by Christ.

2 Thessalonians 3.5

Grace and peace

May grace and peace be yours
in full measure
through your knowledge of God
and of Jesus our Lord.

2 Peter 1.2

Arrow Blessings

God bless you.

James 2.16

Peace be with you.

3 John 15

The Lord be with your spirit.

2 Timothy 4.22

The God of love and peace
be with you.

2 Corinthians 13.11

The grace of the Lord Jesus
be with you.

1 Corinthians 16.23

May God's grace be with you.

Colossians 4.18

May mercy, peace, and love
be yours in full measure.

Jude 2

PRAYERS FOR
GROUP WORSHIP

BUILD US TOGETHER

Prayers for God's people

Lord, make our faith greater.
Luke 17.5

You are

Son of God,
You are the way,
we follow you.

You are the truth,
we trust in you.

You are the life,
we live for you.

John 14.6*

Do not abandon us

Jesus, our Mother:
Do not abandon us
   or leave us empty.
As a hen gathers her chicks
   under her wings,
may your Spirit enfold us,
closer to you, and closer,
in the warmth
   and nourishment
   of your love.

Matthew 23.37,8*

Help us, Lord, and save us!

Lord, you became like us
   and shared our human nature.

Help us, Lord, and save us!

You did this so that through your death
   you might set us free from our
   fear of death.

Help us, Lord, and save us!

You became like us in every way,
   in order to be our faithful and
   merciful High Priest.

Help us, Lord, and save us!

And now you help those who are tempted,
   because you yourself were tempted.

Help us, Lord, and save us!

Hebrews 2.14–18*

Faithfulness

Christ our Lord,
If we have died with you,
   we shall also live with you.

If we continue to endure,
   we shall also rule with you.

If we deny you,
   you also will deny us.

If we are not faithful,
   you remain faithful,
   because you cannot be false
   to yourself.

2 Timothy 2.11–13*

With one voice

May God, the source of patience
  and encouragement,
enable us to have the same point
  of view among ourselves,
that together we may praise
  with one voice
the God and Father
  of our Lord Jesus Christ.

Romans 15.5–6*

Give us the Spirit

Glorious Father!
  God of our Lord Jesus Christ:
Give us the Spirit
  and we will be wise;
reveal yourself to us
  and we will know you;
open our minds
  and we will see your light.

Ephesians 1.17–18*

Build us together

Heavenly Father!
Hold us together
and make us grow
into a sacred temple
dedicated to your Son.
In union with him
build us together
into a place
where you will live
through your Spirit.

Ephesians 2.21–2*

You have loved us

You have called us, O God,
  to be your people.
You have loved us and chosen us
  for your own.
Clothe us with your compassion,
  your kindness, your humility,
  your gentleness and your patience.
Help us forgive one another
  as you have forgiven us.
And bind us all together
  in the perfect unity
  of your love.

Colossians 3.12–14*

Help us to love

Dear Father,
Help us to love one another
with the love that comes from you.
You showed your love for us
by sending your only Son into the world,
that we might have life through him.

Dear Father,
If this is how you loved us,
then we should love one another.
No one has ever seen you,
but if we love one another,
you live in union with us,
and your love in us is made perfect.

Dear Father,
We are sure that we live in union with you
and that you live in union with us,
because you have given us your Spirit,
and you have sent your Son
to be the Saviour of the world.

1 John 4.7–14*

Keep us in your love

We pray, O God,
in the power of the Holy Spirit,
that you will keep us in your love,
as we wait for our Lord Jesus Christ
in his mercy
to give us eternal life.

Jude 20–21*

Arrow Prayers

Lord, teach us to pray.

Luke 11.1

Lord, show us the Father;
that is all we need.

John 14.8

O God, you are the true God.
Keep us safe from false gods.

1 John 5.20–21

Save us, Lord!

Matthew 8.25

Jesus! Master! Take pity on us!

Luke 17.13

Stay with us, Lord:
the day is almost over
    and it is getting dark.

Luke 24.29*

FATHER OF ALL MANKIND

Prayers for God's world

Our Lord, come!
I Corinthians 16.22

Father of all mankind

Father of all mankind:
You are Lord of all;
you work through all;
you are in all.

*Ephesians 4.6**

We look for you

Almighty God,
You have made the world and everything in it.
You are Lord of heaven and earth.
You give life and breath to everyone.
We look for you,
yet you are not far from any one of us.
For in you we live and move and exist.

Acts 17.24–8*

Guide our steps

Merciful and tender God,
Cause the bright dawn of salvation
    to rise on us,
to shine from heaven on all those
    who live in the dark shadow
    of death,
and guide our steps into the paths
    of peace.

Luke 1.78–9*

For all people

O God our Saviour,
To you we offer our petitions,
   prayers and thanksgivings
for all people,
including those who are in
   authority,
that we may live a quiet and
   peaceful life
with all reverence and with
   proper conduct.

1 Timothy 2.1–2*

Make our love grow

May the Lord make our love
　　for one another and for all people
　　grow more and more,
that we may be perfect and holy
　　in the presence of our God and Father
when our Lord Jesus comes
　　with all who belong to him.

*1 Thessalonians 3.12–13***

We cry and weep

Lord, we cry and weep:
help us to see beyond the sadness of
   this hour of suffering,
so that, like a woman about to
   give birth,
we may at last forget the pain
and our hearts may be filled
   with gladness.

John 16.20–22*

Stretch out your hand

Master and Creator of heaven, earth, and sea,
    and all that is in them!
Stretch out your hand to heal,
    and grant that wonders and miracles
    may be performed through the name
    of your holy Servant Jesus.

Acts 4.24,30

How long?

Almighty Lord,
holy and true,
how long will it be
   until you judge the earth?

When will your home be with us?
When will you live with us
   and be with us?
When will you wipe away all tears?
When will there be no more grief,
   no more crying,
   no more pain,
   no more death?

So be it. Come, Lord Jesus.

*Revelation 6.10; 21.3,4; 22.20**

GLORY TO GOD!

Prayers of adoration

To God be the glory
for ever and ever!
Amen.
Galatians 1.5

Glory to God!

Glory to God
 in the highest heaven,
and peace on earth
to those with whom
 he is pleased!

God bless the king
 who comes in the name
 of the Lord!
Peace in heaven
 and glory to God!

Luke 2.14; 19.38

King of kings

To the King of kings
and Lord of lords,
living in the light
that no one can approach –
to him be honour
and eternal dominion!

To the eternal King,
immortal and invisible,
the only God –
to him be honour and glory
for ever and ever!
Amen.

1 Timothy 6.15,16; 1.17*

Glory to the Father and to the Son!

Father,
Give glory to your Son,
   so that the Son may give glory to you.

Glory to the Father and to the Son!

You gave him authority over all mankind,
   so that he might give eternal life
   to all those you gave him.

Glory to the Father and to the Son!

He showed your glory on earth;
   he finished the work you gave him to do.

Glory to the Father and to the Son!

Father,
Give him glory in your presence now,
   the same glory he had with you
   before the world was made.

Glory to the Father and to the Son!

He has made you known to those you gave him,
   He gave them the same glory you gave him,
   so that they may be one, just as you and
   he are one.

Glory to the Father and to the Son!

He in them and you in him,
   so that the world may know that you sent
   him and that you love them as you love
   him.

Glory to the Father and to the Son!

Father,
You have given us to him,
   and we want to be with him where he is,
   so that we may see the glory you gave him;
   for you loved him before the world
   was made.

Glory to the Father and to the Son!

The world does not know you,
   but he knows you, and we know that you
   sent him.

Glory to the Father and to the Son!

He made you known to us,
   and will continue to do so,
   that the love you have for him may be
   in us, and that he also may be in us.

Glory to the Father and to the Son!

John 17.1–6,22–6*

We bless your holy name!

Lord Jesus Christ,
You always had the nature of God,
  but you did not think that by force
  you should try to become equal with God.

We bless your holy name!

Of your own free will
  you gave up all you had,
  and took the nature of a servant.

We bless your holy name!

You became like a man
  and appeared in human likeness.

We bless your holy name!

You were humble
  and walked the path of obedience all
  the way to death – your death on the cross.

We bless your holy name!

For this reason God raised you
  to the highest place above
  and gave you the name that is greater
  than any other name.

We bless your holy name!

And so, in honour of your name
  all beings in heaven, on earth,
  and in the world below
  will fall on their knees.

We bless your holy name!

And all will openly proclaim
  that you are Lord,
  to the glory of God the Father.

We bless your holy name!

Philippians 2.6–11*

God will supply

With all his abundant wealth
    through Christ Jesus,
our God will supply all our needs.
To our God and Father
    be the glory for ever and ever!
    Amen.

Philippians 4.19–20*

A sure foundation

The God of grace,
who calls us to share
   his eternal glory
   in union with Christ,
will himself perfect us
and give us firmness, strength,
   and a sure foundation.
To him be the power for ever!
Amen.

1 Peter 5.10–11*

Let us give glory

Let us give glory to God!
He is able to make us stand firm in
    our faith,
according to the Good News about
    Jesus Christ made known to all nations,
so that all may believe and obey.
To the only God,
who alone is all-wise,
be glory through Jesus Christ
    for ever!
    Amen.

*Romans 16.25–7**

You alone are holy

Lord God Almighty,
   how great and wonderful are your deeds!
King of the nations,
   how right and true are your ways!
Who will not stand in awe of you, Lord?
   Who will refuse to declare your greatness?
You alone are holy.
All the nations will come and worship you,
   because your just actions are seen by all.

Revelation 15.3–4

Praise God!

Praise our God, all his servants
   and all people, both great and small,
   who worship him!
Praise God! For the Lord, our Almighty God,
   is King!
Let us rejoice and be glad!
Let us praise his greatness!

Revelation 19.5–7*

Holy is the Lord

Holy, holy, holy,
is the Lord God Almighty,
who was, who is,
and who is to come.

Our Lord and God!
You are worthy to receive
    glory, honour, and power.
For you created all things,
and by your will
they were given life.

Revelation 4.8,11*

The Lamb who was killed

The Lamb who was killed
is worthy to receive
   power, wealth, wisdom,
   and strength,
   honour, glory, and praise!

To him who sits on the throne
   and to the Lamb,
be praise and honour,
   glory and might,
for ever and ever! Amen.

Revelation 5.12,13

Power to our God!

The power to rule over the world
   belongs to our Lord
   and his Messiah,
and he will rule for ever and ever!

Praise God!
Salvation, glory, and power
   belong to our God!
True and just are his judgements.

Amen! Praise, glory, wisdom,
   thanksgiving, honour,
   power, and might
   belong to our God
for ever and ever! Amen.

Revelation 11.15; 19.1–2; 7.12

To God our Saviour

To him who is able to keep us
    from falling,
and to bring us faultless
    and joyful
before his glorious presence –
to the only God our Saviour,
through Jesus Christ our Lord,
be glory, majesty, might,
    and authority,
from all ages past, and now,
    and for ever and ever!
    Amen.

Jude 24,25*

HOW GREAT IS YOUR LOVE!

Prayers of thanksgiving

Let us thank God
for his priceless gift.
2 Corinthians 9.15

To the merciful Father

Let us give thanks to the God
    and Father of our Lord Jesus Christ,
the merciful Father,
the God from whom all help comes!

2 Corinthians 1.3

Let us give thanks to the God
    and Father of our Lord Jesus Christ!
Because of his great mercy he gave us
    new life,
and filled us with a living hope,
by raising Jesus Christ from death.

1 Peter 1.3*

How great is your love!

God of abundant mercy:
Your love for us is so great.
While we were dead in our disobedience
you brought us to life with Christ.
By your grace you raised us up
to rule with him in the heavenly world.
How great is your love for us
   in Jesus!

Ephesians 2.4–7*

We thank you, our God

We thank you, our God,
   for your love!
You have chosen us to be saved
   by the Spirit's power.
You have made us your holy people
   by our faith in the truth.
You have called us to share
   in the glory of Christ.
We thank you, our God,
   for your love!

*2 Thessalonians 2.13–14**

Let us give thanks!

Let us give thanks
   to the God and Father of our Lord
   Jesus Christ!

Let us give thanks!

For in our union with Christ
   he has blessed us by giving us every
   spiritual blessing in the heavenly world.

Let us give thanks!

Even before the world was made,
   God had already chosen us to be his
   through our union with Christ.

Let us give thanks!

Because of his love
   God had already decided that through
   Christ he would make us his sons.

Let us give thanks!

Let us praise God for his glorious grace,
   for the free gift he gave us in his
   dear Son!

Let us give thanks!

For by the death of Christ we are set free.
   Our sins are forgiven.

Let us give thanks!

Ephesians 1.3–7*

The victory

Thanks be to God
who gives us the victory
through our Lord
  Jesus Christ!

1 Corinthians 15.57

THE LORD BE WITH YOU

Prayers of blessing

*God's grace
be with you all.*
Titus 3.15

The Lord be with you

The grace of the Lord Jesus Christ,
the love of God,
and the fellowship of the Holy Spirit
be with you all.

2 Corinthians 13.13

Peace and love

May God the Father
and the Lord Jesus Christ
give us peace and love with faith.

May God's grace be with all those
who love our Lord Jesus Christ
with undying love.

*Ephesians 6.23–4**

Grace, mercy, and peace

May God the Father
and Jesus Christ, the Father's Son,
give us grace, mercy, and peace;
may they be ours in truth and love.

2 John 3

Goodness and faith

May God make you worthy
   of the life he has called
   you to live.
May he fulfil by his power
   all your desire for goodness
   and complete your work of faith.
In this way the name of our Lord
   Jesus will receive glory from
   you, and you from him,
   by the grace of our God
   and of the Lord Jesus Christ.

2 Thessalonians 1.11–12

Courage and hope

May our Lord Jesus Christ
  and God our Father,
who loved us and in his grace
  gave us unfailing courage
  and a firm hope,
encourage you and strengthen you
  to always do and say
  what is good.

2 Thessalonians 2.16–17

Peace at all times

May the Lord himself,
who is our source of peace,
give you peace
at all times
and in every way.
The Lord be with you all.

2 Thessalonians 3.16

Every good thing

May the God of peace provide you
 with every good thing you need
 in order to do his will,
and may he, through Jesus Christ,
 do in us what pleases him.
And to Christ be the glory for
 ever and ever! Amen.

Hebrews 13.20–21

Freed from our sins

Grace and peace be yours from God,
　who is, who was, and who is to come,
and from the seven spirits
　in front of his throne,
and from Jesus Christ,
　the faithful witness,
　the first to be raised from death.
He loves us, and by his death
　he has freed us from our sins
　and made us a kingdom of priests
　to serve his God and Father.
To Jesus Christ be the glory and power
　for ever and ever!
　Amen.

Revelation 1.4–6

Arrow Blessings

May God our Father
and the Lord Jesus Christ
give you grace and peace.

Romans 1.7

May peace be with all of you
who belong to Christ.

1 Peter 5.14

May peace and mercy
be with all God's people!

Galatians 6.16

May God, our source of peace,
be with all of you. Amen.

Romans 15.33

May the grace of the Lord Jesus Christ
be with you all.

Philemon 25

May the grace of the Lord Jesus
be with everyone.

Revelation 22.21

GOSPEL WORDS FOR CONTEMPLATION

These phrases from the Gospels are for those who wish to include a contemplative element in their prayers. The practice of focusing attention on just one or two of these phrases each day can lead to a deepening awareness of the healing presence of Christ – the Word of God who speaks to the hearts and minds of all who will listen to him intently.

Anyone who is unfamiliar with this way of praying with the New Testament may find it helpful to read chapters 3 and 6 of *Contemplating the Word*, a practical handbook by Peter Dodson (SPCK 1987).

Ask, and you will receive.

Matthew 7.7

Seek, and you will find.

Matthew 7.7

Knock, and the door will be opened to you.

Matthew 7.7

Do you believe that I can heal you?

Matthew 9.28

Come to me . . . and I will give you rest.

Matthew 11.28

Learn from me . . . and you will find rest.

Matthew 11.29

I will be with you always.

Matthew 28.20

Follow me.

Mark 2.14

I have chosen you to be with me.

Mark 3.14

Be still!

Mark 4.39

Be healed of your trouble.

Mark 5.34

Don't be afraid, only believe.

Mark 5.36

What do you want me to do for you?

Mark 10.51

Have faith in God.

Mark 11.22

Be clean!

Luke 5.13

Your sins are forgiven.

Luke 5.20

Your faith has saved you.

Luke 7.50

Where is your faith?

Luke 8.25

Your Father is pleased to give you
the Kingdom

Luke 12.32

God knows your heart.

Luke 16.15

Peace be with you.

Luke 24.36

I am the bread of life.

John 6.35

I am the light of the world.

John 8.12

I am the gate for the sheep.

John 10.7

I am the good shepherd.

John 10.11

I am the resurrection and the life.

John 11.25

I am the real vine.

John 15.1

I am the way, the truth, and the life.

John 14.6

Because I live, you also will live.

John 14.19

You are in me, just as I am in you.

John 14.20

Remain united to me, and I will remain
united to you.

John 15.4

I love you just as the Father loves me.

John 15.9

You will have peace by being united to me.

John 16.33

Stop your doubting, and believe!

John 20.27

Do you love me?

John 21.16

Index
of Biblical References

Praying with

THE OLD TESTAMENT

Compiled by Philip Law

Introduction by Richard Holloway

In this companion volume to the highly praised *Praying With the New Testament*, the words of the Bible are again quoted or adapted in simple, direct prayers to God.

'. . . just what is needed for many people's devotions.'
Hebrew Christian

'a bargain to possess and use'   *Church Times*